HEAR HERE!

HEAR HERE!

by
Trevor Parsons

Illustrations
by
Lucy Creed

Poet and Painter

Poet and Painter

First published as hardback in 2015 by

Poet and Painter

http://www.poetandpainter.co.uk

All poems copyright © Trevor Parsons 2015
Illustrations copyright © Lucy Creed 2015

The rights of Trevor Parsons and Lucy Creed to be identified as the author and illustrator of this work have been asserted by them in accordance with the Copyright, Designs and Patents Act 1988.

ISBN-13: 978-0-9934651-0-9

A CIP catalogue record for this book is available from the British Library.

All rights reserved. No part of this publication may be reproduced, stored in or introduced into a retrieval system, or transmitted in any form or by any means (electronic, mechanical, photocopying, recording, or otherwise) without the prior written permission of the publisher. Any person who does any unauthorised act in relation to this publication may be liable to criminal prosecution and civil claims for damages.

This book is sold subject to the condition that it shall not, by way of trade or otherwise, be lent, re-sold, hired out, or otherwise circulated without the publisher's consent in any form of binding or cover other than that in which it is published and without a similar condition including this condition being imposed on the subsequent purchaser.

For Lan, Jo and Theo
My toughest and most supportive critics

Contents

Cannibals	1
Front of the Class	2
What School's All About	3
A Challenge to Frankenstein	4
Hear here!	5
Are You My Friend or Aren't You?	6
Changes	7
Long Look at a Small Blue Flower	8
All About Poets	9
When is a Thing a Living Thing?	10
Tricky Quiz	11
Christmas Eve in the City	12
Tyrannosaurus rex	13
Funtasy	14
A Polish Folk Tale	16
Love Poem	17
Music While You Do	18
Homophone Fun	20
What Poets Eat For Lunch	21
Seamus	22
Or Is It Nothing?	24
The Teacher's Prayer	26
Before	28
After	29
Playtimes	30
Christmas Limerick 1	32
Christmas Limerick 2	32
Hairy Thoughts	33
Countdown	34
My Word	35
Endangered Species	36

Camouflage?	37
Living with Violence	38
Thaw	39
Somewhere in the Middle	40
Lying Around	41
Ridiculist	42
A Round Tooit	43
Plural Puzzle Poem 1	44
Plural Puzzle Poem 2	44
Something to Aim For	45
My Favourite Pen	46
Lessons of Life	46
An Investigation into Time and Ink	48
Where in the World?	49
The Turkey's Looking Glum	50
School Uniform	52
How It Could Be	54
Pterodactyls	56
When Dinosaurs Kissed	57
The Tyrannosaurs	58
Sounds Strange	60
Are You as Tall as a Story?	61
Lion	62
Sad	62
Sloth	63
Flea School	64
Now I'm Not a Little Kid	66
Best Mate	67
What I Like About Poets	68
Acknowledgements	69

Cannibals

Never give a hand to a cannibal,
even if he looks a bit distressed.
No, never give a hand to a cannibal,
the chances are he'll only want the rest.

And don't lose your heart to a cannibal,
or let him pick your brain – for he might choose it.
Nor, just for fun, should you let one pull your leg,
it might easily come off and you would lose it.

Avoid playing foot ball with cannibals,
it could be one of yours and come to harm.
In short, keep a cannibal at arm's length
and, preferably, use someone else's arm.

Front of the Class

I sit at the front of the class
and try to get on with my work.
The back row are mucking about.

Tom's had a paper dart flown at his head,
it's caught in his hair
and he doesn't know it's stuck there.

He looks like a scoop of ice cream
with one of those horrible fan-shaped biscuits
sticking out the side of it.

I want to laugh out loud
but I suppose I mustn't.
I always have to do the right thing.

Often, when I shouldn't, I just want to be silly,
stop being old Serious Drearious,
or Sternly Burnley - and just be me.

I'm back row material, really I am.
I could mess about with the worst of you,
have a laugh, see the silly side of everything.

It's what I'm like on the inside.
But on the outside it's just not that easy
when you're the teacher.

What School's All About

I go to school to see me mates
and me mates go in for me –
not for a load of histry dates
or boring old poetry,
but to chase around, kick a ball,
cheek the girls who've grown up quick,
chalk nitials on the playground wall
and pick on all the littler kids.

I go to school to muck about
and call out stuff in class,
I try to make our teacher shout
and give me mates a laugh.
I can't stand still in a sembly,
can't even say I've tried,
I like to sing all loud and trembly
and get meself sent outside.

I go to school 'cos they make me;
all round it ain't too bad,
but that litracy and newmracy
don't half get me mad.
Still, mum says they got to be done
so sometimes I read out loud
and a cassionly I do a sum –
but they're not what school's all about.

A Challenge to Frankenstein

Head of a septic boil,
body of a burnt-out car,
chair arms, table legs,
neck of an old guitar.
Golden ears of barley,
eyes from a butterfly's wing,
scraped from last night's custard,
horrible strips of skin.
Cups' lips, shoe's tongue,
teeth of a howling gale,
heart of gold, stomach for a fight,
bottom of a plastic pail.

I know you're very clever
at stitching things together,
but could you make a monster
out of these?

Hear here!

I have felt the window's pane,
sheltered from a tyrant's reign,
made bouquets out of bakers' flours,
made minutes mine that should be hours.
I've jousted with the starlit night,
built a castle on the sense of sight,
moored my schooner to a front door key,
stirred two sugars in a golfer's tee.
I've seen the twitch of a fairy tale,
the colour of death in a cheap tin pail,
felt the pulse of a weather vane,
been a sailor on a stallion's mane.
I've known the saviour of a leather sole,
buttered both halves of an actor's role,
caught a ball by a royal throne
and I have heard the long grass mown.

Are you my friend or aren't you?

Are you my friend or aren't you?
I don't think friendship's a game.
Monday, we queued up for chips after school,
Today you're giggly with Jane.

Are you my friend or aren't you?
Will I ever know anyone well?
You laughed yesterday at the joke I made,
Today you laughed when I fell.

Are you my friend or aren't you?
How to tell truth from a lie?
On Tuesday you lent me your best felt-tipped pens,
Now I just can't catch your eye.

Are you my friend or aren't you?
There are so many things I don't know.
Where does the sun set, the East or the West?
How do I stop feeling low?

Are you my friend or aren't you?
You've made things so hard I can't guess.
Perhaps it's a question I wouldn't be asking,
If the answer was, yes.

Changes
(Reversible and Irreversible)

Falling out with Freddie
was like water freezing into ice,
chocolate melting, sugar
dissolving in tea.
We apologised, patched things up
and got back together –
the ice thaws, chocolate sets,
sugar is left as the tea dregs dry.

Falling out with Nick though
was different. We couldn't forgive
and forget,
it was clay firing to china, the decay
of dead animals, a cake cooked,
the rich coal burning to ash.
No going back.

Long look at a small blue flower

I have to tell you
the sun's come out and so too the lobelia
and it's so blue it steals my breath away.

It's bluer than the bluest, most beautyfullest eyes,
it's bluer than aeroplane window skies.
It's bluer by far than far mountain ranges,
bluer than budgerigars preening in cages.
Bluer than bluebells or ink-stained paper,
bluer than the ocean around Jamaica.
Bluer than a peacock's hundred 'eyes',
bluer than flashy baboons' backsides.
Bluer than a sapphire or a stripe of rainbow,
bluer than light through a stained glass window,
bluer than the flash of a kingfisher's wings,
bluer
        than the sum of all these things.

Look closer in, each small flower's like
an amazingly fine, exotic kite.
I wonder, could such sublime perfection
have simply evolved for bee attraction?

All About Poets

A poet is for life
not just for Christmas Day.
Stroking a silky-haired poet
can soothe your troubles away.

A long-haired breed of poet
should always be kept well-groomed.
Keep their sleeping-quarters
in a draught-free part of the room.

Do not indulge your poet
with titbits from your plate.
Encourage regular exercise
to avoid excessive weight.

It is generally thought unhealthy
to have poets in your bed.
Be sensitive about disposal
once your poet is dead.

Sorry, I meant to say 'pet'.

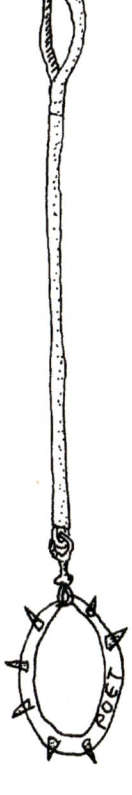

When is a Thing a Living Thing?

If a thing is living it will move
however far or fast or slight,
a falcon swooping on a shrew,
the turning of a leaf to light.

All living things can reproduce,
remake themselves as young and new,
the growing of a rose from seed,
your mother giving birth to you.

A living thing must feed or die
so bats go hunting moths at night,
sheep must graze and insects nibble
and green plants conjure food from light.

And life means growth, things getting bigger,
from tiny sapling to enormous tree,
from foal to horse, from calf to cow,
you, from what you are to what you'll be.

Tricky Quiz

Can you surf on a microwave?
Can a saxophone be engaged?

How far can a front door step?
Why is a vacuum cleaner?

How long can a music stand?
How deep did the kitchen sink?

Which is louder – cold tap or hot?
How many rounds can a window box?

Just how far can a cricket pitch?
How fast can the sugar bowl?

Why is electric light?
Why is a cigarette lighter?

Christmas Eve in the City

No sign of snow
but down wary streets
a sharp wind roams.
The rich slumber
on their pocket-sprung mattresses
while the homeless cramp
on their orthopaedic pavements.
The bellies of the rich
swill with fine wines,
the bellies of the homeless
grind on handouts.
Beneath the trees of the rich
the presents seem endless.
Beneath the tree of the homeless
the present seems endless.

Tyrannosaurus rex
(after "Ozymandias" by Percy Bysshe Shelley)

I found some fossils in a desert land.
There were two vast unbroken lengths of bone,
once legs that strode, and by them, in the sand,
a massive shattered skull whose size alone
spoke of a beast of fiendish strength and speed
who would, with ease, outrun, outfight all prey.
A mighty jaw ablaze with fearsome teeth,
the socket of an eye that once surveyed
all lesser creatures with a cold disdain.
It was Tyrannosaurus rex, whose name
has rung down history as King of Kings –
yet I, not he, have lived to find such things.
Around this monument to his demise
the telling sands of time stretch to the skies.

Funtasy

Once upon the plains of Afridia
a gentleman elephant was alumphing
across the grassland of the savannah
when he found himself facing
a beautiful lady tiger.
Far from fighting
and much against the laws of nature
they fell in love and soon were mating
and, in the fullness of pregnancy, had
a baby elephantiger – a fabulous beast,
with moist black trunk, stripy hide
and murderous, razor-sharp teeth.

Once upon several years later,
whilst fanning himself with his huge furry ears,
the virile young elephantiger
found a gorgeous young gerbil had strayed near.
She was small but beautifully formed.
'Size is no barrier,' the pair agreed
and soon they had dated and mated and so were born
a dozen elephantigerbils, a breed
the like of which our world has never seen.
Smallish, roundish, bewhiskered, tusked,
striped with fur and rumpled skin,
a nose much more than snout yet not quite trunk.

And then a plague of locusts had turned the noon to dusk,
descended on the land, stripped it bare and flown.
But one female elephantigerbil could not believe her luck,
for one male locust had decided to remain.
What a catch he was - film star looks,
six strong legs, a fine figure of an insect,
and once again, against all odds
an ill-matched pair just clicked
and bred. And so the elephantigerbilocusts became.

One day, one of the above,
relaxing after some youthful energetic game,
met a turtleopardingostrichicken –
an extraordinary beast, almost beyond imagination.
And soon was born, as a consequence of love,
a monster with a very long name.

A Polish Folk Tale

Once upon a time, in Lodz, in Poland,
a girl met a young man who was tall and
bald, while she was as short as water
in a drought and as hairy as a Rasta.
He liked to stay in, read books and play chess,
she preferred to party in a shocking red dress.
How different they were, but against all the odds
they married and lived happily, in Lodz.

Once upon another part of Poland
a tall and gorgeous girl met a tall and
gorgeous guy. They both loved dancing and wine
and thought untidiness a dreadful crime.
They were healthy, wealthy and none too
wise – you'd expect them to love long and true.
So much in common and yet their first night
was also their last. It was loathe at first sight.

The moral of this story
works for magnets just as well;
opposite Poles attract
while similar Poles repel.

Love Poem

I love chocolate in the morning,
I love chocolate after noon,
I'd love some chocolate later
and I'd love some chocolate soon.

I love it when I'm hungry,
I love it when I'm not,
and chocolate's great in winter,
in a mug, and piping hot.

I love chocolate when it's milky,
when it's white and when it's plain,
but the sort of chocolate I love best
is the sort I can have again.

I exercise to beat the flab
and I floss to stop the rot,
but I'm up against one simple fact –
I'm in love with choc a lot!

Music While You Do

There's music on the radio
        for music while you work,
there's music at the dentist's
        for music while you're hurt,
there's music in your headphones
        for music while you walk,
there's music at the party
        for while you dance or talk.

There's music on the TV show
        for music while you view,
there's music in the restaurant
        for music while you chew,
there's music in the lift
        for music while you rise,
there's music in the motorcar
        for while you doze or drive.

There's music on the telephone
>   for music while you wait,
there's music at the ice rink
>   for music while you skate,
there's music in the shopping mall
>   for music while you buy,
there's music in the chapel
>   for music when you die.

There's music, music everywhere,
>   on every film they make;
there's music, far more rarely,
>   just for music's sake.

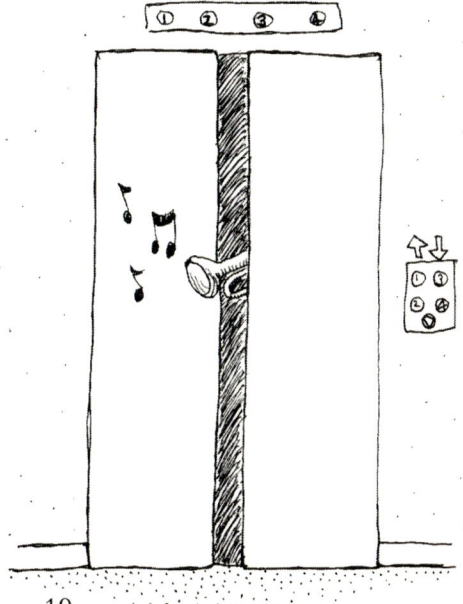

Homophone Fun

Uncle Ted said, "Let's shoot bear,"
and went to fetch his gun.
Auntie Jess heard, "Let's shoot bare,"
and thought it might be fun.

Pete said he was, "a little hoarse,"
but would sing if he was able.
John heard him say, "a little horse,"
and thought him quite unstable.

If anyone should offer you
some after dinner mints,
make sure they mean the chocolate type
not after dinner mince.

"Look at the size of my mussels,"
said the diner to his guest.
She flinched, for she'd heard "muscles"
and hoped he wouldn't undress.

"My prints!" the lady thief cried out –
she'd forgotten to wear her gloves.
But the young detective heard "My Prince!"
and wondered, "Could this be love?"

What Poets Eat For Lunch

Around 1 o'clock, when they're ready for lunch,
poets decide on which sandwich to munch.
Some always go for fillings that rhyme
forgetting that taste should come first every time.
So lamb may be chosen with soft bits of clam
or ham thickly smothered with cranberry jam.
A bap or a wrap with slivers of gammon
with frogs' legs, ducks' eggs and the roe of a salmon.
Salami, pastrami and a nice bit of brisket,
fat from a rat and a sprinkling of biscuit.
Lychees and cheese with a garnish of fleas –
all the above are quite likely to please.

Other poets, time after time,
choose alliterative fillings, rather than rhyme.
So tiny tomatoes, tuna and tongue,
lugworms and lentils with lemon and lung,
Brussels, baloney, bananas and beet -
any of these would be right up their street.

Mind you, some are less fickle,
liking pickle and free verse

Seamus
(with apologies to Seamus Heaney)

'Looks like your hamster's had it then,'
my older brother yelled upstairs.
I two-at-a-timed it down –
he'd been alright at eight,
breathing a bit like a bellows
but then, with the sun on his cage…
and he was getting on.

Outstretched, uncovered, on his sawdust pile,
he lay like a cutlet on a bed of rice.
His eyes were black ink drops, surprised,
that seemed to stare beyond outside.
I could see he'd gone. I used to pet him,
never caring that he'd bite or scratch,
but now, his stillness, I dared not touch.

The tiny paws looked embryonic, pink and clean,
and though I could have stroked them, didn't –
respect, or something like it, I suppose.
At last, breath held, I picked him out,
about as bulky as a bundled sock,
more limp, already barely warm,
and stared. Alive at eight o'clock; dead at nine.

I'd missed his death.
I guess he died unnoticed,
much as, most of the time, he'd lived.
Died while the breakfast things were put away.
I made his coffin from a cardboard box
some eighteen centimetres long.
Eighteen – one for every month.

Or is it nothing?

Did I see that shadow shiver
underneath the freezer door?
Does that long brown curtain quiver
where it hangs down to the floor?
Or is it nothing?

Is there something in that corner
of the hallway by the stairs?
I thought I heard it hold its breath -
see the way the darkness stirs.
Or is it nothing?

Lying in my bed I have that
'Is someone in my bedroom?' feeling.
What's that sound like tickling paper
coming from above the ceiling?
Or is it nothing?

Do I hear a tiny scratching
from the shelves behind my back?
Those patterns in the sugar bowl –
do they make a kind of track?
Or is it nothing?

Dad's looking pleased.
I think he whispered "caught" to Mum,
seems keen to get a half-filled bin bag
out before the bin men come.
Or is it nothing?

The Teacher's Prayer

Please grant to us a holiday
that lasts throughout the year
with bags of extra salary
to enjoy not being here.

Or failing that I'd settle for
a slightly shorter day,
let's say from ten to half past twelve
with one hour off for Play.

Or failing that I wouldn't mind
if all my class had flu.
I might let one child struggle in
but I'd draw the line at two.

Or failing that, please could our Head
forget her way to school,
and end up somewhere miles away –
like Thailand or Peru.

Or failing that, please might I miss
my dreaded Playtime Duty,
especially if it's cold and wet
when all the kids are naughty.

Or failing that I'd love to find
the books upon my shelf
are a massive stack of homework
that's magically marked itself.

If none of this is possible
I pray my class will sit
and listen, thrilled, to my fine words
when the School Inspectors visit.

Before

Before is party poppers, boxed.
A lit match moving to a rocket.

Before your friends turn up, your room
listens to music.

Before is a brand new door,
your hand upon its handle.

Before the storm, the tallest trees
shiver with expectation.

Before you read it, a book
is every book you haven't read.

Before the sun explodes tomorrow, today
will be like any other.

After

After the parked car drove off in the rain
a dry patch remained, like an abandoned shadow.

After your friends had all gone home
your room tingled with silence.

After being lost for words, that night
words overcrowded in.

After teacher left the room, like a control
the closing door turned up the volume.

After the storm, fallen leaves
gathered to whisper their stories.

After your very last chance, sometimes,
may come another.

Playtimes

are for playing in,
racing round and chasing in,

calling, screaming, shouting out,
making friends and falling out,

tripping, slipping, kneecap scraping,
even arm and leg bone breaking,

bouncing, throwing, Frisbee flinging,
at the tops of voices, singing,

chalking risky words on walls,
in high gutters, losing balls,

playing football, passing, hogging,
hopscotch hopping, leapfrog frogging,

releaster, cricket with a stick,
dreading when the teams get picked,

"Fight! Fight!" crowding round,
two boys scrapping on the ground,

staying in when outside's wet,
teachers cross and kids upset,

if it's icy, sliding, skating,
under summer sunshine, baking,

cheeking some poor dinner lady,
holding Sally's mum's new baby,

losing coats, forgetting lunches,
older girls in giggling bunches –

but, if you're new or on your own,
there's no worse time to feel alone.

Christmas Limerick 1

When Santa had loaded his sleigh
and was ready to get on his way,
his wife held him back,
said, "Put on this mac.
I'm sure there'll be rain, dear, today."

Christmas Limerick 2

There once was a greedy young elf
who kept Santa's gifts for himself.
He made quite a name
for in time he became
an elf of exceptional welf.

Hairy Thoughts

Hair is mighty remarkable stuff
for, considering its thinness,
it's surprisingly tough.

Why should armpits sprout thick hair,
and the private bit down there?
They're rarely exposed to freezing air!

As people get old their hair gets bold.
A nostril or earhole, once a smooth area,
eventually gets outrageously hairier.

Hair on a fish in the Arctic Sea
seems a far better place for hair to be
than clothing an ape in a tropical tree.

Countdown
(Why are the most sensible things so often wrong?)

Ninety

Eighty

Seventy

Sixty

Fivety

Fourty

Threety

Twoty

Onety

Nonety

My Word

starts with a letter in fourth but not author,
its second you'll find in fifth but not froth,
its third is in third but is not there in thinned,
the fourth is in second but never in conned,
the fifth is in sixth but not in six hundred.
The whole wins the race, is what comes before all.

answer: my word is first

Endangered Species

I'm an endangered animal
though nobody cares
for I don't have cute eyes
or strokeable hair.
I'm not thrilling to look at
like a cheetah at speed,
I can't snatch your breath
like a chimp in tall trees.
I haven't the razor sharp eyes of an eagle,
I haven't the radar-like ears of a bat,
I don't have the heart-melting voice of a songbird,
can't even repel like a sewer bred rat.
But I have got a life
- small hopes and fears too –
and I'd quite like a future,
if it's alright with you.

Camouflage?

Zebras' stripes are made from pipes
of black and white, and flattened,
then tightly wrapped around their backs
in a most outstanding pattern.
This is odd because the stripes, we're told,
are there so they can't be seen,
but zebras live in the hills and plains
which are not black and white, but green.
And how to explain an okapi,
who just has stripes on his rear,
surely those stripes are not simply there
to make his bum disappear?

Living with Violence

Mothers, otherwise kind, drag carpets outside
and beat them in Springtime;
they tie-up laces and punch cushions into shape.
In empty afternoons time is killed,
sorrows are drowned on sad occasions
and unwanted Christmas gifts heartlessly flogged.
In the kitchen, the hub of the family,
olives are stoned and eggs beaten,
fish battered and cream whipped.
Salt is pinched, cakes cut
and potatoes routinely mashed.
The squeezing of lemons is rife,
oranges have their skins peeled
and toast is randomly burnt.
Elsewhere, letters are stamped,
matches struck, umbrellas shaken;
old wallpaper is forcibly stripped
and the new rolls given a pasting.
Paintings are hung, curtains drawn
and sandwiches quartered.
A mouse gets dragged across a mat
while favourite web-sites are repeatedly hit.
After New Year bad habits may be kicked
and promises, at any time, broken.
Notes get pinned to the wall,
old books have their spines cracked
and worn clothes onto floors are mindlessly thrown.
It's a vicious, violent place – the home.

Thaw

Tree leaves drip like overflows,
and things on lawns, like submarines,
surface darkly in the soft white sea.
Roofs slip then avalanche,
snowmen lose their confidence and shrink,
while tiny bird foot patterns grow.
Droplets of sunlight.
Silence melts.
Everydayness is being returned -
though not where shadows
slumber in their plumped white beds.

Somewhere in the Middle

Won't get A's, won't star in plays,
won't shine in sports or school reports,
no music skills to give a thrill,
won't ever be
the one you see
applauded as a prodigy.

But won't bunk school, won't kick the rules,
won't get in fights or stay out nights,
won't rob or mug, won't deal in drugs,
won't be the one
your dad or mum
would make you stay away from.

Not dull, not bright, but still alright,
don't need to be extraordinary.
Not damned as worst, not praised as best
but don't forget me
or neglect me –
there's more of me than all the rest.

Lying Around

Lying on the beach
lying in the sun
lying on a lounger
lying having fun.
Lying by the water's edge
lying in the foam
couldn't go to school that day
lying ill at home.

Lying in department stores
lying, she was caught
lying in a cell before
lying in the court.
Lying to the magistrate
she was nowhere near the crime
lying she was on the beach
lying all the time.

Ridiculist

Fetch me a slice of confetti,
a fistful of Norwegian wine,
and buy me a pinch of spaghetti
with a punnet of light bulbs, size nine.

Remember to order a packet of eggs
and a small reel of lard, while you're there;
I fancy a gallon of tiny frogs' legs
and a surfeit of something that's rare.

And let's have a bale of electrical juice
and a sliver of grit – if they have it -,
a sachet of screws of no possible use
and one inch of one foot of one rabbit.

Finally, find me a tall bunch of rock
and a dozen of best belly-fluff -
here, take all the coins I've left in my sock,
I hope you won't find it's enough.

A Round Tooit

Before he starts jobs round the house
a round tooit is something dad needs.
Square tooits, or oblong, are no use at all,
"When I get a round tooit," he pleads.

Sometimes he may need "half a mo"
instead of, or as well as, the tooit;
but never a full mo, or a mo and a half,
and we haven't a clue how he'd use it.

If he can't get his mo or his tooit
we usually have a long wayt,
and though mum says short wayts are better
they're just not the sort that dad makes.

Dad often won't do what he's asked to
but will make complete ballzups instead -
unlike the mo, the ballzup is whole,
a thing only found undivided.

Once dad has completed his ballzup,
it's mum's turn, to make a t'doo.
Her t'doo is always a right one –
I've not heard of a left one, have you?

Plural Puzzle Poem 1

What colour are
rhinoce roses?
The hippopota
muses.

Plural Puzzle Poem 2

Is it because
the ant elopes,
the porcu
pines?

Something to Aim For

Everyone I know has thrown up,
even the Queen must sometimes spew,
but though we've all done Farmhouse Soup,
I like to be sick in a single hue.

I did a brilliant purple once
on the back seat of our car
after a heavy Ribena session,
and a road too twisty by far.

And once on a cross channel ferry
I chucked up in orange as well –
a carrot and coriander special
brought on by the heavy swell.

I did a mushy pea green sick
on my best friend's kitchen floor
and an amazing tomato and red pepper job
that ran down our bathroom door.

I've puked up yellow and I've puked in pink
but up to now I've never spewed blue.
The bringing up is easy,
any country drive will do,
but what should I eat, that's the problem –
or should I just cheat and drink
ink?

My Favourite Pen

My favourite pe

Lessons of Life

My favourite pen has just run out of ink.
Now I am using another one which
is not so pleasing but does the job.
It teaches me not to rely on things.

Things will always let you down, sometime.
But it also teaches me to carry a spare
if I don't want to get caught out.
Which is why I try to wear two watches,

two pairs of underpants and four socks.
In hot weather it can get quite uncomfortable
and this teaches me that compromises
must often be made. Often

I compromise with the pants and quite often
with the socks. This also teaches me
that mothers are usually right because
mine said I wouldn't last long with all those clothes on.

Sadly, I cannot get a refill for my favourite pen
because they do not make them anymore.
This is very annoying but teaches me
that you can't always get what you want

and that nothing stands still,
even in the world of pens and refills.
I think I should also learn not to become
too attached to material things but maybe I should learn

that it's okay to be attached to things
but don't expect them to last – a variation of
all good things come to an end.
Which is a very big lesson of life.

I suppose I have also learnt that
lessons of life can sometimes contradict each other,
which is yet another lesson of life.

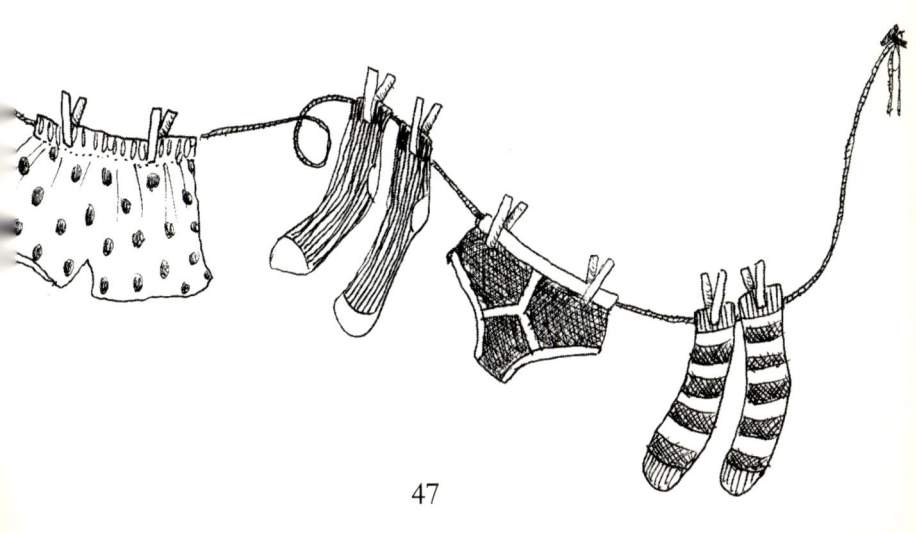

An Investigation into Time and Ink

I I ev ot vr scn lte cn o sil nesad ht hv witn?
If leve ut vey tir lete ca yo stll ndrsan wht I av wrttn?
If I eav out ver fouth ltte can ou sill ndestad wht I hve wittn?
If I lave ot evey fifh leter ca you sill udersand wat I hve wrtten?
If I leve out very sxth leter ca you stll undrstan what I ave wrtten?
If I leae out evry seveth lettr can yo still uderstad what I ave writen?
If I leav out ever eighth ltter can ou still nderstad what I hve writtn?

In cocluson I bliev my exerimnt shws tht anyne ca save ime an ink b leavng ou ever fifh leter an stil be unerstod.
Or mybe ven ver fouth.
But I on't tink m expeimen is vey scintifc.

Where in the World?

Where in the world does tomorrow
come before yesterday?
Where does the past follow future
and August come before May?

And where on Earth would you find
a cart in front of a horse,
and where does three come way after four
while fifth comes just before fourth?

answer: in a dictionary

The Turkey's Looking Glum

Christmas is coming,
the turkey's looking glum,
I think he's got an inkling
of the fate that is to come.

Christmas is coming,
Mum is getting snappy,
far too much to do, she says,
which makes her far from happy.

Christmas is coming,
shop assistants cringe,
working twice as hard to cope
with each year's shopping binge.

Christmas is coming,
fir trees glancing round,
looking out for muscly men
who'll chop them to the ground.

Christmas is coming,
postmen bending low
under tons of Christmas cards
whizzing to and fro.

Christmas is coming,
bin men start to fear
the trillion tons of wrapping
we chuck away each year.

Christmas is coming,
kids all shout hooray,
for all that's wrong we wouldn't have it
any other way.

School Uniform

If *we* have to wear a uniform
then the teachers should have to too –
something they'd never wear outside of school
and so grim it could hardly be true.

Clothes they would not be seen dead in,
that would make a model look drab,
a style which was never in fashion
and sported a pompous gold badge.

I see seams picked out with piping
and I'd favour ridiculous stripes
in a clashing selection of colours
which would give any stomach the gripes.

Their footwear should also look stupid,
maybe sandals rather than shoes
and not in a colour they'd normally wear
but one that an infant would choose.

Then people would know they were teachers
on trips or just travelling to school
and policemen could easily trace them
for fighting or spray-painting walls.

Of course, I know what would happen,
they'd start messing their uniforms up.
They'd be untucking shirts or rolling up skirts
or wearing their hats back to front,

and soon every one would look different,
as un-uniform as can be
because teachers are, apparently, human
beings like you and like me.

How It Could Be

You say that you can't stand assemblies -
well, what if they lasted all week?
And say they were pitch dark and freezing
with a Head who did nothing but shriek?

And though you believe Maths is boring,
just think if your teacher had said,
"Count all the specks on this filthy old floor
and divide by the hairs on your head."

Imagine how awful, in English,
having to learn and recite
the complete works of Shakespeare backwards
until you got every word right.

In P.E. your teacher turns nasty
and insists that you go for a jog –
up the M1 in the blazing hot sun
while dragging a twenty foot log.

The school dinner ladies have grabbed you,
force gallons of stew down your throat;
it's made from the skin of old custard,
rubbish dump slime and a stoat.

If going to school makes you shudder,
remember the words of this verse –
however bad you think it might be
IT COULD BE VERY MUCH WORSE!

Pterodactyls

Some say the Pterodactyl never flew
while others think it did.
The ones who say it couldn't fly
claim it only glid.

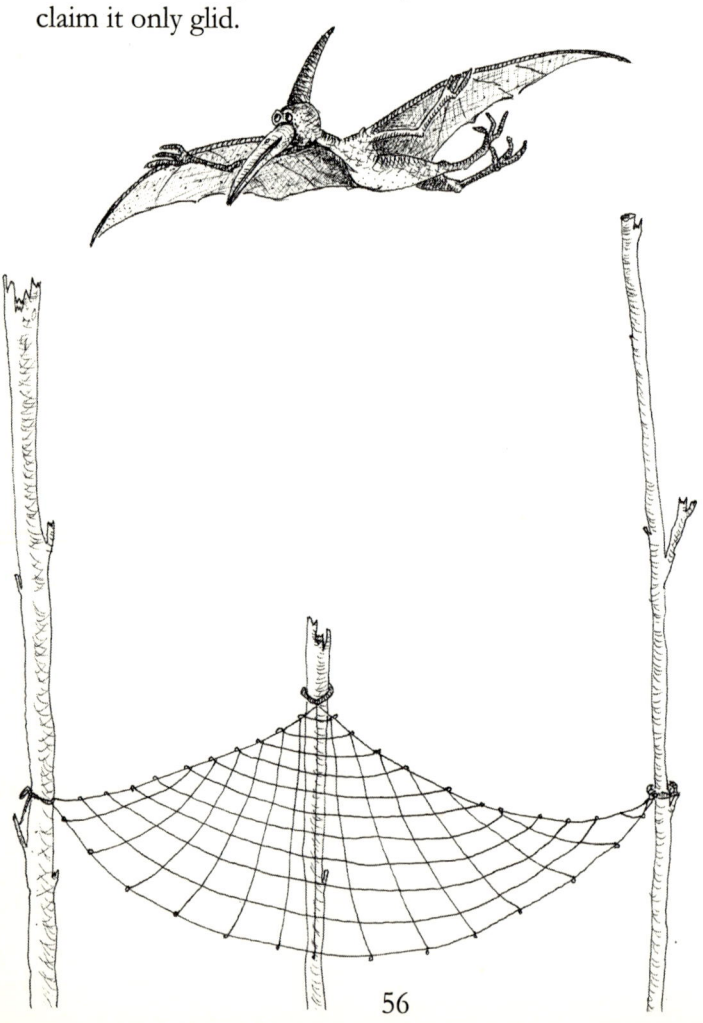

When Dinosaurs Kissed

When dinosaurs kissed
the crash of their lips
was a noise that all learned to fear,
for the spittle and drool
would drown any fool
who was silly enough to stand near.

When they danced face to face
in a torrid embrace
tectonic plates would start shaking,
and the scrape of their scales
was quite like when nails
down faces of blackboards are raking.

When dinosaurs cuddled
and nibbled and nuzzled
small creatures got squashed on the ground.
It has to be said,
when such romance was dead,
there were primeval cheers all around.

The Tyrannosaurs

Tyrannosaurus rex
was big and bold and strong
but also had a brother,
Tyrannosaurus ron.

Rex was really vicious
and liked to kill and stuff.
Ron liked books and flying kites
and shrank from looking tough.

Rex would snatch small mammals
to chew as finger food.
Ron found them rather friendly
and thought his twin plain rude.

And then into their lives,
with loud, blood curdling roar
stomped a wicked, hungry, cross
and vast Giganotosaur.

Rex was up for fighting
and tried to claw him down,
but his own bloodied body soon
lay lifeless on the ground.

Ron - who saw it all and knew
clever does what clever can –
sized up the situation and
Tyronnosaurus ran.

Sounds Strange

The tick, tick, ticking of your teacher's pen,
as loud as a school report,
the bark of a tree, the boom of a crane,
the tread of a tractor's tyre,
the ring around an index finger,
the racket set up by a confidence trickster,
a note to remind, a sink's cold tap,
the narrow squeak of escape,
the call of the sea, metal grating,
the buzz you get when you score,
a bottle of pop, the hum of poo,
the chink of light round a door.

Are You as Tall as a Story?

Are you as tall as a story
or as short as having no cash,
are you as thin as dishwater soup
or as fat as a lip that's been bashed?
Are you as strong as the smell of manure,
as weak as a feeble excuse,
when you run do you run like paint or a nose,
do you exercise like books?
Is your skin as smooth as a salesman
or as rough as a gang-load of thugs,
are you as bright as a halogen light,
as dense as an old London smog?
Are your eyes as green as a new recruit
or as blue as a very sad tune,
do you love like a zero in tennis,
do you pine like a tree in the woods?
Will you study as well as a hole in the ground,
will you bring up your children like sick,
will your life be spent like a penny
and lost in the wash like a sock?

Lion

By and large,
When a lion
Is by
And large
And rough and ready
For his scoff,

You're better
Off!

Sad

The toucan do
what you can do
but alas
the pelican't.

Sloth

Algae grows on his coat
Because he moves so slowly.
Because he moves so slowly he
Needs little to eat.
Will hang rather than stand,
Sleeps mostly, pees weekly,
Drinks never – leaf juice and dew
Are enough.
Says hardly more than a breath.
Perhaps sloth is practising
For death.

Flea School

How irritating fleas can be –
yet they're not like it naturally,
but have to learn to stab and bite
and feast upon our blood at night
and though the average flea's no fool
that flea, like you, must go to school.
Their schools are held in filthy vests,
in underpants and hairy chests.
They're taught by lice who, by and small,
are really not that nice at all
but treat the fleas like little pests,
and try to be the cruellest.
The Head louse and her Deputy
are also horrid to the fleas
and will expel, when feeling mean,
a lazy flea to somewhere CLEAN.
This school life lasts a single day,
just long enough to learn the way
to multiply and use their strength
to jump a hundred times their length,
how to dodge the scraping finger,
and drive one mad but never linger
underneath a squashing thumb.

The Head, when Graduation comes,
urges all to do her bidding -
find some spot to scratch a living,
somewhere squalid, somewhere dark
and, though microscopic, make their mark.

Now I'm Not a Little Kid

I can't believe I used to think
there were such things as beasts
that prowled with blood-red, killer's eyes
the forests of our sleep,
nor monsters formed from Devil's touch
or by a witch's spell,
nor creatures foul and hideous
that found their way from Hell.
There's nothing much that scares me now,
I think I'm pretty tough
and though I look beneath my bed,
it's just to check for dust.

Best Mate

We're best mates – the sort of mates you see
arms round shoulders, round each other's houses,
all the time. When the going gets tough
he stays, says 'Fantastic' if I win a race,
would always pick me first for teams.
He's not the sort to gloat at my defeats,
wouldn't talk behind my back, top my stories
or drone on about his parents' bigger house
or posher car. He wouldn't blank me to look big,
or block me from a group and would always share
his homework, the last slurp of his Irn Bru.
He's great. He's my best mate.
I just wish it were true.

What I like about Poets

What I like about poets
(though I've not met many)
is that you can bump into them
in dark alleys or soccer stands
and they won't punch your lights out
(unless hopelessly drunk).
And they're not known for being
drop-dead gorgeous,
which would make you feel ugly
and envious;
or filthy rich,
which would make you feel poor
and envious;
or revoltingly ambitious,
which would make you feel
trampled on and annoyed;
or loud, boasty show-offs
(unless hopelessly drunk),
which would make you feel
overshadowed, unappreciated and cross.
And I like the way (so I've heard)
that they all love words
and between them have written those fewish poems
without which
my life would be so much thinner.

Acknowledgements

The author is grateful to the editors of the following collections where these poems first appeared:

'Front of the Class' in *Read Me At School*
edited by Gaby Morgan, Macmillan 2009

'Are You My Friend or Aren't You?' in *Poems for my Best Friend*
edited by Susie Gibbs, OUP 2004

'All About Poets' in *The Jumble Book*
edited by Roger Stevens, Macmillan 2009

'When is a Thing a Living Thing?' in *Read Me At School*
edited by Gaby Morgan, Macmillan 2009

'Tricky Quiz' in *I Say, I Say, I Say*
edited by John Foster, OUP 2003

'What Poets Eat for Lunch' in *Let's Recycle Grandad*
edited by Roger Stevens, A&C Black 2008

'The Teacher's Prayer' in *The Teacher's Revenge*
edited by Brian Moses, Macmillan 2003

'Playtimes' in *The Poetry Store*
edited by Paul Cookson, Hodder Children's Books 2005

'Christmas Limericks 1&2' in *Funny poems for Christmas*
edited by Paul Cookson, Scholastic 2005

'My Word' in *The Universal Vacuum Cleaner*
edited by John Foster, OUP 2005

'Something to Aim For' in *Revolting Rhymes*
edited by Susie Gibbs, OUP 2006

'Where in the World?' in *Puzzling Poems*
edited by Susie Gibbs, OUP 2006

'Now I'm Not a Little Kid' in *Monster Poems*
edited by Brian Moses, Macmillan 2005